Black Writers

A BOOK OF POSTCARDS
Photographs by Jill Krementz

POMEGRANATE ARTBOOKS
SAN FRANCISCO

Pomegranate
Box 6099
Rohnert Park, CA 94927

Pomegranate Europe Ltd.
Fullbridge House, Fullbridge
Maldon, Essex CM9 4LE
England

ISBN 0-7649-0022-6
Pomegranate Catalog No. A865

Pomegranate publishes books
of postcards on a wide range of subjects.
Please write to the publisher for more information.

Designed by Elizabeth Key
Printed in Korea

07 06 05 04 03 02 01 00 99 98   12 11 10 9 8 7 6 5 4 3

To facilitate detachment of the postcards from this book, fold each card along its perforation line before tearing.

Black Writers

PHOTOGRAPHS BY JILL KREMENTZ

RITA DOVE, Charlottesville, Va., March 4, 1995

Rita Dove (b. 1952) has won numerous awards for her verse, including a Pulitzer Prize for *Thomas and Beulah* (1987), a story-poem about her grandparents. In 1993 she was appointed U.S. Poet Laureate, becoming the youngest poet and the first African American to receive this honor.

POMEGRANATE   BOX 6099   ROHNERT PARK CA 94927

Black Writers

PHOTOGRAPHS BY JILL KREMENTZ

ALEX HALEY, New York, N.Y., September 24, 1976

Alex Haley (1921–1992) was responsible for two of the most influential books of contemporary times. From interviews, papers, and speeches, he wrote *The Autobiography of Malcolm X* (1965), and from genealogical and historical research, he wrote *Roots: The Saga of an American Family* (1976). *Roots* was translated into twenty-six languages and won 271 awards, including a Pulitzer Prize.

POMEGRANATE BOX 6099 ROHNERT PARK CA 94927

Black Writers

PHOTOGRAPHS BY JILL KREMENTZ

A. J. VERDELLE, Brooklyn, N.Y., March 1, 1996
A. J. Verdelle (b. 1960) made an immediate impact on the literary scene
with her debut novel, *The Good Negress* (1995), which won wide praise and
was a finalist for the PEN/Faulkner Award. A graduate of the University of
Chicago, Verdelle founded and operates a successful consulting company
in New York, Applied Statistics & Research.

POMEGRANATE BOX 6099 ROHNERT PARK CA 94927

Black Writers

PHOTOGRAPHS BY JILL KREMENTZ

NTOZAKE SHANGE, New York, N.Y., June 16, 1976
Ntozake Shange, playwright, poet, and novelist, was born Paulette
Linda Williams in 1948. She took her African name—meaning "she
who walks like a lion"—to help fight "a war of cultural and esthetic
aggression." Among her award-winning works are *For Colored Girls
Who Have Considered Suicide, When the Rainbow Is Enuf* (1975),
Sassafrass (1976), *Nappy Edges* (1978), and *Liliane* (1994).

POMEGRANATE BOX 6099 ROHNERT PARK CA 94927

Black Writers

PHOTOGRAPHS BY JILL KREMENTZ

WOLE SOYINKA, Stockholm, Sweden, May 1973
Wole Soyinka (b. 1934) was the first African to win the Nobel Prize
in literature. A poet, playwright, and novelist, he has unflinchingly
chronicled the turmoil of modern postcolonial Nigeria as well as
his own traditional Yoruban culture. Following threats on his life by
Nigeria's ruling military regime, Soyinka left that country in 1994 and
became a spokesman for the return of democracy there.

POMEGRANATE BOX 6099 ROHNERT PARK CA 94927

Black Writers

PHOTOGRAPHS BY JILL KREMENTZ

CONNIE BRISCOE, Falls Church, Va., February 15, 1996
Connie Briscoe added a fresh new voice to contemporary fiction with her debut novel, *Sisters & Lovers* (1994), a witty and instructive tale of three sisters living in Washington, D.C. Her literary gifts were reaffirmed in the best-selling *Big Girls Don't Cry* (1996). Deaf for most of her adult life, Briscoe is former managing editor of *American Annals of the Deaf* at Gallaudet University.

POMEGRANATE BOX 6099 ROHNERT PARK CA 94927

Black Writers

PHOTOGRAPHS BY JILL KREMENTZ

VERONICA CHAMBERS, New York, N.Y., June 4, 1996
Veronica Chambers (b. 1970) turned her singleminded desire to be
a writer into a rite of passage and an act of redemption, capturing
both in her spellbinding debut, *Mama's Girl* (1996). A memoir of
her Brooklyn childhood, the book also chronicles her swift rise in the
literary world, which includes her former editorial position at the
New York Times Magazine.

POMEGRANATE BOX 6099 ROHNERT PARK CA 94927

Black Writers

PHOTOGRAPHS BY JILL KREMENTZ

SONIA SANCHEZ, Philadelphia, Pa., March 14, 1996

Sonia Sanchez (b. 1934) is a poet, playwright, and professor (at Temple University) who has committed herself to political progressivism since the 1960s. She has written and edited numerous volumes, including *We a Baddddd People* (1970), *We Be Word Sorcerers: 25 Stories by Black Americans* (1973), and *A Blues Book for Blue Black Magical Women* (1974).

POMEGRANATE BOX 6099 ROHNERT PARK CA 94927

Black Writers

PHOTOGRAPHS BY JILL KREMENTZ

JOHN EDGAR WIDEMAN, Amherst, Mass., November 5, 1995
John Edgar Wideman (b. 1941) is one of America's most inventive writers, using a complex mix of techniques to create "an elaborate poetic portrait of the lives of ordinary black people." A former basketball star and Rhodes scholar, Wideman won the PEN/Faulkner Award for *Sent For You Yesterday* (1984). His other works include *Reuben* (1987), *Philadelphia Fire* (1990), and *All Stories Are True* (1992).

POMEGRANATE BOX 6099 ROHNERT PARK CA 94927

Black Writers

PHOTOGRAPHS BY JILL KREMENTZ

NIKKI GIOVANNI and JAMES BALDWIN, New York, N.Y., March 17, 1974
Nikki Giovanni (b. 1943) and James Baldwin (1924–1987) were two of the
strongest and most provocative literary voices of the 1960s. Baldwin's *The
Fire Next Time* (1963) was a powerful indictment of racial tyranny, while
Giovanni's impassioned verse established her as one of America's best-
loved poets before she turned thirty. She now teaches at Virginia Tech.

POMEGRANATE BOX 6099 ROHNERT PARK, CA 94927

Black Writers

PHOTOGRAPHS BY JILL KREMENTZ

TERRY McMILLAN, New York, N.Y., April 29, 1995

Terry McMillan (b. 1951) is an uninhibited and wildly funny writer whose tales of manners among modern African American women *(Disappearing Acts, Waiting to Exhale)* have quickly achieved mass success. She is also in demand for her enthralling readings of her work.

POMEGRANATE   BOX 6099   ROHNERT PARK CA 94927

Black Writers

PHOTOGRAPHS BY JILL KREMENTZ

HENRY LOUIS GATES JR., New York, N.Y., May 9, 1994
Henry Louis Gates Jr. (b. 1950) is one of America's most prolific and
brilliant critics as well as a leader in African American scholarship. He is
editor of and contributor to numerous volumes of critical essays, slave
narratives, and series of rediscovered classics of African American literature and is the author of a best-selling memoir, *Colored People* (1994).

POMEGRANATE   BOX 6099   ROHNERT PARK CA 94927

Black Writers

PHOTOGRAPHS BY JILL KREMENTZ

ALICE WALKER, New York, N.Y., March 11, 1974
Alice Walker (b. 1944), the daughter of a Georgia sharecropper, has
become one of America's most prominent literary figures. She is author
of eleven books of poetry and prose, including the semiautobiographical
The Third Life of Grange Copeland (1970) as well as *Meridian* (1976) and
the Pulitzer Prize–winning *The Color Purple* (1982).

POMEGRANATE BOX 6099 ROHNERT PARK CA 94927

Black Writers

PHOTOGRAPHS BY JILL KREMENTZ

ISHMAEL REED, Berkeley, Calif., March 22, 1974
Ishmael Reed (b. 1938) has, from his first novel, *The Free-Lance Pall-bearers* (1967), and his first book of poetry, *Conjure* (1972), been a provocative presence in contemporary writing. His work is filled with tricks of time and typography, voodoo, Egyptian symbolism, satire, and invective. A collection of his best essays, *Writin' Is Fightin'*, was published in 1990.

POMEGRANATE BOX 6099 ROHNERT PARK CA 94927

Black Writers

PHOTOGRAPHS BY JILL KREMENTZ

MAYA ANGELOU, Winston-Salem, N.C., April 14, 1994
Maya Angelou (b. 1928), poet, playwright, and professor, has said, "I speak to the black experience, but I am always talking about the human condition." This was made clear to millions when she read one of her poems at President Bill Clinton's inauguration. Her autobiographical prose and poetry have been collected in several volumes, including *I Know Why the Caged Bird Sings* (1970).

POMEGRANATE BOX 6099 ROHNERT PARK CA 94927

Black Writers

PHOTOGRAPHS BY JILL KREMENTZ

ANNA DEVEARE SMITH, WALTER MOSLEY,
and GLORIA NAYLOR, New York, N.Y., July 28, 1994
Playwright and actor Anna Deveare Smith (b. 1950), mystery writer and
novelist Walter Mosley (b. 1952), and novelist Gloria Naylor (b. 1950)
are pictured here at the 1994 "Spoken Word" series held on Central
Park's SummerStage.

POMEGRANATE   BOX 6099   ROHNERT PARK, CA 94927

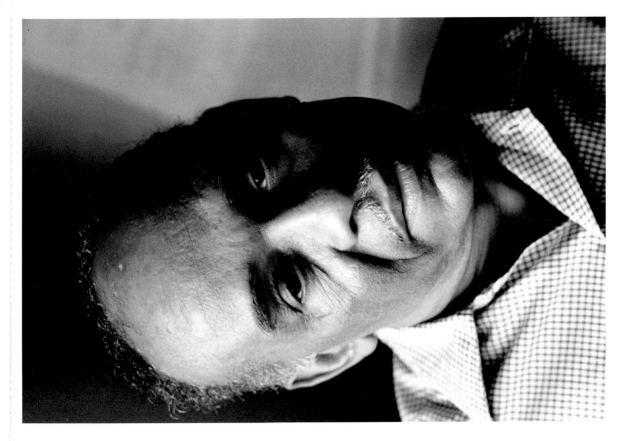

Black Writers

PHOTOGRAPHS BY JILL KREMENTZ

RALPH ELLISON, New York, N.Y., June 21, 1973
Ralph Ellison (1914–1994) was one of America's most influential post-war writers, author of the novel *Invisible Man* (1953) and the essay collections *Shadow and Act* (1964) and *Going to the Territory* (1987). He saw literature as a "raft of hope" needed to sail through the "snags and whirlpools that mark our nation's vacillating course toward and away from the democratic ideal."

POMEGRANATE BOX 6099 ROHNERT PARK CA 94927

Black Writers

PHOTOGRAPHS BY JILL KREMENTZ

DOROTHY WEST, Oak Bluffs, Martha's Vineyard, Mass., April 28, 1995
Dorothy West (b. 1907) moved from Boston to New York as a young
woman and became an integral part of the Harlem Renaissance in the
1920s. She founded two magazines, *Challenge* and *New Challenge,* as
outlets for African American writers. At age eighty-seven, she published
the acclaimed novel *The Wedding* (1994).

POMEGRANATE BOX 6099 ROHNERT PARK CA 94927

Black Writers

PHOTOGRAPHS BY JILL KREMENTZ

DEREK WALCOTT, New York, N.Y., January 18, 1986
Derek Walcott (b. 1930) won the Nobel Prize in literature in 1992,
becoming the first native Caribbean to be so honored. "In him," stated
the Academy, "West Indian culture has found its great poet." A brilliant
scholar and thinker, Walcott has taught at Columbia, Harvard, and Yale
Universities and has written numerous volumes of poetry and plays.

POMEGRANATE BOX 6099 ROHNERT PARK CA 94927

Black Writers

PHOTOGRAPHS BY JILL KREMENTZ

DORI SANDERS, Charlotte, N.C., April 3, 1994
Dori Sanders (b. 1934) was raised on her family's peach farm in York County, South Carolina, which is still in operation. Her first novel, *Clover* (1990), draws on that setting to create an instantly memorable tale of race relations in the modern South. Her second novel, *Her Own Place* (1993), was equally well received.

POMEGRANATE BOX 6099 ROHNERT PARK CA 94927

Black Writers

PHOTOGRAPHS BY JILL KREMENTZ

STANLEY CROUCH, LEON FORREST, ALBERT MURRAY,
and JAMES ALAN McPHERSON, New York, N.Y., May 26, 1994
The influential writers Stanley Crouch (b. 1945), Leon Forrest (b. 1937),
Albert Murray (b. 1916), and James Alan McPherson (b. 1943) are pictured here paying homage to a mentor and generous friend, Ralph
Ellison, following a memorial service at the American Academy of Arts
and Letters.

POMEGRANATE   BOX 6099   ROHNERT PARK CA 94927

Black Writers

PHOTOGRAPHS BY JILL KREMENTZ

GWENDOLYN BROOKS, New York, N.Y., November 13, 1993
Gwendolyn Brooks (b. 1917) has earned, with her gently insightful poetry,
some fifty honorary degrees, a Pulitzer Prize for *Annie Allen* (1949), the
Illinois Laureateship (succeeding Carl Sandburg), and the Consultantship
in Poetry at the Library of Congress. She still lives near where she grew
up—the South Side of Chicago, the setting for much of her verse.

POMEGRANATE   BOX 6099   ROHNERT PARK CA 94927

Black Writers

PHOTOGRAPHS BY JILL KREMENTZ

JAMAICA KINCAID, New York, N.Y., November 27, 1995
Jamaica Kincaid, born Elaine Potter Richardson in St. John's, Antigua, in 1949, has crafted five critically acclaimed books that rediscover and transform her coming of age in the West Indies. Her novels *Annie John* (1985) and *Lucy* (1990) gained Kincaid a wide readership, and *The Autobiography of My Mother* (1996) propelled her to the best-seller list.

POMEGRANATE BOX 6099 ROHNERT PARK, CA 94927

Black Writers

PHOTOGRAPHS BY JILL KREMENTZ

ANN PETRY, Old Saybrook, Conn., March 12, 1996
Ann Petry (b. 1908) grew up in Old Saybrook, Connecticut, where her
family ran the local drugstore. In 1938 she moved to Harlem, attended
Columbia University, and began writing fiction. Her first novel, *The Street*
(1946), was a stunning debut and is now regarded as an American classic.
Her later novels *Country Places* and *The Narrows* were set in New England,
to which she returned in 1948.

POMEGRANATE BOX 6099 ROHNERT PARK CA 94927

Black Writers

PHOTOGRAPHS BY JILL KREMENTZ

ERNEST GAINES, San Francisco, Calif., March 13, 1975
Ernest Gaines (b. 1933) was raised in the rich black culture and story-
telling tradition of rural Louisiana but was deeply influenced by Russian
writers such as Chekhov, Gogol, and Turgenev. The "austere dignity" of
his prose has filled six novels, including *Catherine Carmier* (1964), *The
Autobiography of Miss Jane Pittman* (1971), and, most recently, *A Lesson
Before Dying* (1993).

POMEGRANATE   BOX 6099   ROHNERT PARK, CA 94927

Black Writers

PHOTOGRAPHS BY JILL KREMENTZ

TONI MORRISON, New York, N.Y., February 13, 1974
Toni Morrison (b. 1931) creates richly textured prose that mines her experience as an African American woman in a predominantly white society. For her entire body of work—from her first novel, *The Bluest Eye* (1970), through *Jazz* (1992)—she was awarded the 1993 Nobel Prize in literature.

POMEGRANATE BOX 6099 ROHNERT PARK CA 94927

Black Writers

PHOTOGRAPHS BY JILL KREMENTZ

ROBERT HAYDEN, Washington, D.C., October 27, 1976
Robert Hayden (1913–1980) was the first African American to be named
Consultant in Poetry (now Poet Laureate) at the Library of Congress.
His poetic voice, rooted in black experience, had a universal vision that
resounded with power in such works as *A Ballad of Remembrance* (1962)
and *Words in the Mourning Time* (1970).

POMEGRANATE BOX 6099 ROHNERT PARK CA 94927

Black Writers

PHOTOGRAPHS BY JILL KREMENTZ

BELL HOOKS, New York, N.Y., October 3, 1995
bell hooks (b. 1952) was born Gloria Watkins but took the name of
her great-grandmother (written without capitalization) to "honor
the unlettered wisdom of her foremothers." Professor hooks, in her
numerous books of essays, has provoked and challenged women with
insights into race, gender, and class in America. Among her works are
Ain't I a Woman: Black Women and Feminism (1981) and *Sisters of
the Yam* (1993).

POMEGRANATE BOX 6099 ROHNERT PARK CA 94927

Black Writers

PHOTOGRAPHS BY JILL KREMENTZ

DARRYL PINCKNEY, New York, N.Y., October 18, 1995
Darryl Pinckney (b. 1953) is an award-winning critic, essayist, and novelist whose witty, brilliant, and lyrical prose has been called as good as any now being written in English. His picaresque debut novel, *High Cotton* (1992), was lauded for its excruciating honesty and total freedom from restraint.

POMEGRANATE BOX 6099 ROHNERT PARK CA 94927

Black Writers

PHOTOGRAPHS BY JILL KREMENTZ

EDWIDGE DANTICAT, Brooklyn, N.Y., July 11, 1995
Edwidge Danticat (b. 1969) began publishing her stories at age four-
teen, soon after arriving in the United States from Haiti. Her debut
novel, *Breath, Eyes, Memory* (1994), quickly established her presence,
and *Krik? Krak!* (1995) confirmed her promise, earning a nomination
for the National Book Award.

POMEGRANATE BOX 6099 ROHNERT PARK CA 94927

Uncompromising and thorough in her preparation, Jill Krementz brings to each session a familiarity with her subject's work. This sensitivity allows her, according to one reviewer, "to convey her subject's literary style as well as that person's physical image."

Of the ten million Africans who survived transportation as slaves, there are now about one hundred million descendants, mostly in the United States and the West Indies. Several generations removed, the chroniclers of this diaspora have found the pen to be mightier than the chains that once bound their ancestors. With impressive results, African American and West Indian writers are voicing on paper the trials and triumphs of those descendants, provoking, reminding, warning, and stimulating the world's readers. The thirty images of African American writers contained herein were selected by the photographer as the most representative from her sessions with those subjects. ■

As a young woman, Jill Krementz (b. 1940) quickly established herself as one of America's most talented photojournalists. Even while cutting her teeth as a reporter, columnist, and photographer for various New York–based publications—including the *New York Herald Tribune*, which hired her in 1964 as its first female (and youngest) staff photographer—Krementz displayed a passionate and unique visual style.

Now the author of more than two dozen award-winning books—including the "Very Young" and "How It Feels" series for children and young adults—Krementz has long had a special affinity for writers. Although this developed quite naturally from her lifelong love of reading, what began as a bibliophile's attempt "to carve out a little niche for myself" has grown into a massive, and unrivaled, photographic archive of contemporary literary figures. Dating back to 1961 and comprising sessions with more than 1,200 writers, her collection is not just a visual feast for modern book lovers; it will also serve as an invaluable resource for future scholars, not unlike Carl Van Vechten's photographic collection of Harlem Renaissance writers of the 1920s and 1930s.